LUFTWAFFE AT WAR

German Rocket Planes

The BP 20 M17 was completed on 13 December 1944 and tested a few days later on 29 December 1944 on the Heuberg. After the *Steilstart* (vertical take-off) had been proved possible with the BP 20 M16, the M17 was fitted on the launching ramp. Instructions were printed on the fin for anyone finding this unmanned *Wunderwaffe* (wonder weapon) to inform the military headquarters of the *Truppenübungsplatz* Heuberg immediately.

LUFTWAFFE AT WAR

German Rocket Planes

Manfred Griehl

Greenhill Books
LONDON

Stackpole Books
PENNSYLVANIA

Greenhill Books

This edition of *German Rocket Planes* first published 2000 by Greenhill Books, Lionel Leventhal Limited, Park House, 1 Russell Gardens, London NW11 9NN www.greenhillbooks.com
and
Stackpole Books, 5067 Ritter Road, Mechanicsburg, PA 17055, USA

British Library Cataloguing in Publication Data
Griehl, Manfred
German Rocket Planes. – (Luftwaffe at war; v. 14)
1. Rocket planes – Germany – History 2. World War, 1939–1945 – Aerial operations, German
I. Title
940.5'44'943

ISBN 1-85367-404-4

Library of Congress Cataloging-in-Publication Data available

Designed by DAG Publications Ltd
Designed by David Gibbons
Layout by Anthony A. Evans
Printed in Singapore

GERMAN ROCKET PLANES

With the Allied introduction of round-the-clock bombing – by the USAAF during the day and the RAF at night – the complete destruction of the German Reich seemed inevitable. It became obvious to the *Luftwaffe* High Command (OKL) that they must seek effective ways to protect key German industries as well as important targets against enemy action with a minimum of effort.

The general dispositions of the *Luftwaffe* in the West during the period leading up to the Allied invasion of Normandy had already made it clear that fighter forces belonging to *Jagdkorps* I and II deployed all over occupied France and in Germany were too weak to hinder Allied raids. Only some 170 single-engined day fighters together with some 145 twin-engined destroyers could be put into the air to stop enemy raids over Western Europe.

By early September 1944 the air situation in the West could scarcely have deteriorated further. Day fighter formations had no chance of recovering their former strength, although, in September 1944, the German aircraft industry reached the peak of its effort in the production of Bf 109G and Fw 190A fighters and fighter-bombers. This allowed the operational units of the *Luftwaffe* to build up to a combat strength never before achieved. But the severe losses of well-trained fighter pilots and crews together with the lack of fuel hindered the OKL in defending Germany from the air.

Heavy losses among the *Luftwaffe* led to improved plans to defend important targets with the help of small, single-seat target-defence fighters. The first twelve Me 163B rocket-propelled fighters, called *Komet*, had been delivered to *Erprobungskommando* (EK) 16, an evaluation and testing unit for rocket-propelled aircraft, early in January 1944. At last the first rocket-powered *Komet* aircraft were available some two years after the roll-out of the Me 163B V1, the first prototype

of the B series. Until then, the sole Me 163 belonged to the A series and was only used for training purposes, although trials had been carried out to evaluate armament installations.

After *Hauptmann* Wolfgang Späte's test flights with both the Me 163A and B, several other *Luftwaffe* officers and NCOs joined the training programme. Among the first thirty was *Feldwebel* Alois Wörndl, an experienced *Luftwaffe* fighter pilot. During take-off for his first 'sharp' start – a powered start using the rocket motor, rather than a towed take-off – the fuel supply was spent. The rocket engine stopped and Wörndl's Me 163B exploded killing the pilot who was found with his neck broken.

Late in the War, one Me 163 was also tested with R4M rockets fixed beneath both wings in a programme established for the *Reichsverteidigung* (defence of the Reich), the improvement of the Me 262's armament with heavier guns or self-stabilised rockets and remote-controlled air-to-air missiles.

A limited number of the Me 163A, formerly designated as Bf 163 in order to camouflage the new design, were delivered to the *Luftwaffe* for training purposes. The first prototype – the Me 163A V4 – featured the aircraft code KE+SW. It was followed by a limited number of As not all of which were powered by a rocket system; most of them were unpowered gliders used for training.

Early in 1944 the *Luftwaffe* commenced training with the new rocket-powered aircraft whose propulsion system was extremely sensitive and likely to explode if both components of the fuel, called *C-Stoff* and *T-Stoff*, came into contact.

The first combat-ready aircraft, the Me 163B V14 (VD+EW), arrived at Zwischenahn in January 1944 and was flown by Rudolf Opitz who simulated an operational mission at 24,000 ft. By 31 January 1944 the first Me 163 *Staffel* with twelve Me 163s was subordinated to the command of *Luftflotte*

Reich. First it was a part of JG 1 and received the designation of 20./JG 1. Only one month later the unit was renamed 1./JG 400 commanded by *Oberleutnant* Robert Olejnik.

In March 1944 the first aircraft armed two 30 mm MK 108 cannon was sent to Zwischenahn to be evaluated. On 21 April 1944 Robert Olejnik broke his back in a crash landing. During that time a second *Staffel* was raised, equipped with twelve Me 163s. The EK 16 still existed and was responsible for evaluating the series Me 163 with a fixed armament under combat conditions.

Together with Rudolf Opitz, Wolfgang Späte also trained the pilots assigned to EK 16 and prepared them for their first 'sharp' start. Most of the seventy early Me 163Bs produced had been handed over to EK 16 and belonged to the Me 163B-0 or the B-1 series. The first pre-series aircraft had been fitted with two MG 151 guns. From the forty-seventh *Komet* it was proposed to install the more powerful MK 108 guns. Due to a shortage of weapons the *Luftwaffe* was forced to use the 20 mm MG 151 guns until early 1945.

The first combat action occurred on 13 May 1944 when *Major* Wolfgang Späte tried to shoot down a P-47 over northern Germany; Späte's rocket fighter went too fast, broke the sound barrier and overshot his intended victim. The next attempt was carried out by Rudolf Opitz flying the Me 163B V33 (GH+IL). Due to lack of fuel he was forced to land before engaging Allied aircraft. On 20 May 1944 *Oberfeldwebel* Nelte, another member of EK 16, took off with his Me 163B V40 in response to a scramble but no contact with enemy aircraft was reported. Some other interceptor missions were carried out until Allied heavy bombers launched a bombing attack on the EK 16's base at Zwischenahn on 30 May 1944. In June 1944 the OKL ordered a halt to further attacks until more Me 163s were available. The operational use of the Me 163Bs recommenced one month later when *Unteroffizier* Schiebeler tried to shoot down a P-38 on 7 July 1944.

Meanwhile, in Wittmundhafen and Venlo, Me 163 *Staffeln* were established to intercept Allied bombers on their way to the Ruhr region. From 10 July 1944 the second and third *Staffeln* both belonging to I./JG 400 were sent to Brandis where a strong combat unit was established with radar support and enough *C-Stoff* and *T-Stoff* to carry out defensive missions. The first B-17 was shot down by *Leutnant* Hartmut Ryll at the end of July 1944. On 16 August 1944 three Allied aircraft were shot down by *Leutnant* Hans Bolt and *Feldwebel* Schubert and *Feldwebel* Strassnicky. *Leutnant* Ryll's fighter was hit by a P-51.

After another, unconfirmed, victory near Venlo by 1./JG 400 early in August 1944, the unit was transferred to Brandis on 6 September 1944. Two days later the *Führungsstab* of the OKL declared that the Me 163 was now fully operational and ordered the establishment of four new *Staffeln* (4., 5., 6. and 7./JG 400). These were equipped with Me 163B rocket fighters, thus forming a second *Gruppe*, II./JG 400.

After *Leutnant* Schreiber had damaged an Allied bomber and forced it to drop out of formation, he shot down another bomber on 11 September 1944 – the seventh kill of 1./JG 400. Two days later the 2./JG 400 carried out nine unsuccessful interception missions. Early in October 1944, some thirty Me 163s were available at Brandis, near Leipzig where one of the most important industrial regions was situated. But Allied bomber streams bypassed the area and it was impossible for the Germans to intercept them.

During that time Robert Olejnik's unit, the (replacement) *Ergänzungsstaffel* of JG 400 was enlarged to a third *Gruppe* (III./JG 400) of the sole rocket fighter *Geschwader*. It was ordered by the OKL to set up two more *Staffeln*. The units were transferred to Udetfeld. Pilot training was concentrated near Gelnhausen where all available Me 163As, some Me 163 gliders and a few fully equipped Me 163B-1 fighters were gathered. During the final stages of flight training the men were supposed to fly some 15 hours with the rocket fighter before passing on to the combat formations of JG 400. During that time the lack of fuel hindered the second *Gruppe* of JG 400 and only a limited number of interception missions were attempted. Only a few experienced pilots were chosen to take off.

On 20 and 30 November heavy bombers of the 8th Army Air Force headed to Brandis and industrial targets around this *Luftwaffe* base. During that time I./JG 400 had thirty-one Me 163s with nine ready for action. Parts of the unit were sent to Stargard near Stettin to protect an important refinery. There were nine rocket fighters stationed there, of which four were operational. On 12 December 1944 the units based near Stettin were redesignated 5. and 6./JG 400 and formed the nucleus of II./JG 400. At the end of 1944 *Major* Wolfgang Späte returned from Russia and started to form the *Geschwaderstab* of JG 400. Späte became the first *Geschwaderkommodore* of the sole rocket fighter *Geschwader* comprising three *Gruppen* each planned to be of four *Staffeln*.

Due to the Russian advance in January 1945 Udetfeld was evacuated and the III. *Gruppe* was moved to Sprottau, then to Brandis where some 100 Me 163s were dispersed in the woods surrounding the fighter base. The II. *Gruppe* was far from any noteworthy activity in the air. Only a few interception missions were carried out from Zwischenahn and from Brandis. But in March 1945 the JG 400 pilots claimed three B-17s downed, but these kills were credited to Me 262 pilots.

After it became obvious that Allied ground forces would shortly reach Brandis it was evacuated. On 16 April 1945 the base was captured by the 60th Armoured Infantry Battalion which found some 300 aircraft, mostly destroyed, standing in formerly well-camouflaged boxes built nearby.

The production of the Me 163 was considered to be a total of some 360 of 454 projected aircraft, of which more than 433 were estimated to be ready for delivery before January 1945. Between May and September 1944 no more than fifty-five to sixty-five Me 163Bs were manufactured by Messerschmitt and under licence by the Klemm works at Böblingen. During the last month it proved impossible to deliver enough Me 163s as ordered by the *Reichsluftfahrtministerium*. Due to the lack of both experienced engineers and workers, the number of Me 163s produced was small. By Summer 1944 many of the firms that were part of the Me 163 programme received more specialists to build this top-secret fighter. By 27 September 1944 only sixteen series aircraft had been handed over to the *Luftwaffe*. Thirteen others had been given to *Bauabnahme Luft* which was responsible for all standards and equipment ordered by the *Reichsluftfahrtministerium*. By 1 October 1944 the ordered output was reached by the manufacturers. Some sixty-one aircraft were completed in October 1944. Some ten to twenty Me 163s were manufactured but were not completely ready for delivery. During these weeks, unsuccessful attempts to finish sixty incomplete Me 163 fighters at Oranienburg were made, so that they might become part of the monthly delivery. In November 1944 only twenty-two Me 163s were handed over to *Luftwaffe* units.

A handful of Me 163Bs were retained by the factory that built them and flown by the works' own test pilots rather than delivered to the *Staffeln* of JG 400. To increase the number of series aircraft *General der Jagdflieger* Adolf Galland ordered the works to concentrate on completing the *Einflugbetrieb* (the last check before transferring the fighters to a combat unit) at the airfield of Sorau. The task was carried out by Junkers' own pilots and ground specialists. By 31 December 1944 some thirty of more than sixty Me 163s had been sent to Sorau (code name 'Antonienhof') to carry out final

test fights before the rocket fighters saw action with JG 400 around Leipzig.

Due to the concentration of manpower and more specialists being engaged in Me 163 production some eighty-nine Me 163Bs were produced in December. In January 1945 some thirty Me 163s were completed followed by only three aircraft in February and four in March 1945. Plans to develop a more powerful version of the Me 163 and the development of the Me 263, a rocket fighter with two separate combustion chambers, were stopped. Only a few prototypes had been built by the time of the unconditional surrender.

Besides the Me 163/263, a second projected rocket-powered fighter was considered. Only a few attempts to develop new rocket-propelled variants of the Me 262 were undertaken in Lechfeld near Augsburg in Bavaria by early 1945. This development was named the Me 262C. The first design was classed as an interceptor, later redesignated *Heimatschützer* (Homeland protector) I to III. Early in 1945 three different conversions based on the Me 262A-1 had been worked out but only two were tested in flight a few times.

The first Interceptor designs were delivered to the *Reichsluftfahrtministerium* during early summer 1943. The descriptions of the new type, a Me 162A-1a with an additional rocket propulsion unit in the rear fuselage, combined the range of the jet fighter and the extreme climb rate of a rocket fighter. Due to difficulties with the first prototype which was damaged by Allied bombs on 12 September 1944 and many technical problems with the installation of the R II 211/3 unit in the tail unit of the Me 262, the first take-off was delayed. On 27 February 1945 the industrial pilot Lindner first took off with the help of two Jumo jets and the additional Walter (HWK) rocket propulsion. Due to the bad weather and sand found in the rocket system the Messerschmitt evaluation department was forced to overhaul the Me 262C-1a once more. The second trial happened on 16 March 1945. After two more tests the damaged prototype, called *Heimatschützer* I, was captured by Allied forces on 20 April 1945.

The second rocket-propelled Me 262 variant named *Heimatschützer* II based on the Interceptor II was worked out during the course of 1943. The aircraft called the Me 262C-2b was powered by two BMW TLR (*Turbinenluftstrahltriebwerk mit Raketenantrieb*) engines which consisted of a BMW 003 jet on which a liquid-fuel BMW P 3390 rocket system was installed. Early in 1944 some ground trials with the new propulsion system were carried out. The first experimental aircraft was not constructed earlier than December 1944. Again many technical difficulties hindered Messerschmitt but after changing major parts following an explosion in one composite nacelle a final test was carried out on 23 March 1945. The first TLR flight was carried out by *Flugkapitän* Baur on 26 March 1945. After 40 seconds the pilot shut down the rocket motor and returned to Lechfeld. On 12 April 1945 work on the *Heimatschützer* II was stopped, the aircraft was rebuilt as a standard Me 262A-1a fighter and was transferred to a *Luftwaffe* jet-fighter *Gruppe*.

The Me 262C-3 was developed early in 1945. A jettisonable rocket system was fixed beneath the fuselage of an Me 262. The propellant was housed in tanks suspended from the forward fuselage bomb racks. A mock-up of this variant was found by Allied troops at Oberammergau in Bavaria.

In addition to all of the Messerschmitt rocket fighter designs, the Me 163s, 263s and Me 262Cs, a small independent aircraft constructor tried to develop its own design, supported by *Reichsführer SS* Heinrich Himmler and his *SS-Wirtschaftshauptamt*. This small wooden aircraft was ready to enter active service with the *Luftwaffe* (or SS) during the closing weeks of World War II. The general design of the Bachem Ba 349 *Natter* (Viper) had been worked out in late summer 1944. It was possibly first proposed as an manned, single-seat suicide aircraft with a heavy shell fixed in front of the small cockpit. Initially a solid-fuel rocket motor was suggested but later this was replaced by a liquid-fuel motor. The pilot lay in a prone position and could attack with nine RZ 65 rocket batteries grouped in the nose of the Bachem Project (BP 20) which was also called *Bemannte Rakete* (manned rocket) *Berak* I. Late in September 1944 the proposals were altered into a proposal called *Natter*, a small wooden aircraft fitted with a Walter rocket motor and four S 34 boosters.

Together with the *Deutsche Forschungsanstalt für Segelflug* (DFS) and several small factories, the Bachem *Werke* in Waldsee started to develop the new fighter with the help of the SS. First, trials were conducted with unpowered manned and unmanned prototypes. At the *Luftwaffe* airbase at Neuburg on the Danube, the Bachem *Werke* together with the DFS joined to test the flight characteristics of the new fighter aircraft. Some experimental *Nattern* were towed by an He 111 H-6 to a height of 7,500 ft. The first manned *Natter* (Ba 349 M1) was tested with limited success on 3 November 1944. The pilot left the aircraft using his parachute. The *Natter* was completely destroyed when

it crashed. The second manned aircraft (Ba 349 M3) was fitted with an undercarriage but was also slightly damaged during landing at Neuburg. One other prototype (M2) was destroyed during a flight test at Ainring. Two more prototypes followed.

The first vertical take-off was tried on 18 December 1944. The unmanned experimental *Natter* (Ba 349 M21) was completely destroyed after it caught fire on the launching ramp. It was followed by M16 which was also destroyed. The next prototype (M17) left the ramp and was later used for drop experiments because the fuselage showed minor damage after landing with the help of a large recovery parachute.

These tests were followed by nine more but unmanned tests occurred between the end of December 1944 and 24 March 1945. The sole manned vertical take-off was carried out by the former *Leutnant* Lothar Sieber, who had been demoted to *Gefreiter* by order of a court martial at Minsk on 11 February 1943. On 22 December 1944 *Gefreiter* Sieber moved to Bachem and became an industrial pilot. After watching some of the experimental take-offs at the Neuburg, the young pilot entered the Ba 349 M23 on 1 March 1945. The experienced pilot probably lost orientation and he tried to escape after jettisoning the glazed cabin hood but before he could bail out the M23 hit the ground and was wrecked. Lothar Sieber was killed in the accident. After this no other manned take-off was carried out. After testing the Ba 349 M25 on 2 April 1945, the unmanned *Natter* was launched on 10 April 1945 from one of the launching ramps in the restricted area on the Heuberg near Stetten am kalten Markt.

A final attempt to test the *Natter*'s operational opportunities was called 'Sonderaktion Krokus'. The SS ordered that fifteen manned *Natter* aircraft be available by 1 March 1945 for an attack on Allied bombers over southern Germany. Wooden launching ramps were installed but the first operational use of the new weapon was delayed too long. The remaining *Natter* aircraft were brought to Bad Wörishofen and a cave near Füssen, both in Bavaria. Later a few of them were captured by Allied soldiers in Sankt Leonhard and components were captured by the Soviets in Thuringia and at the proving grounds at Tarnemünde.

Despite a lot of manpower and material the development of target-defence fighters did not achieve any worthwhile results in action due to their limited range and hazardous methods of operation which involved high explosive fuel for take-off.

Some twenty-five Me 163Bs were captured in Germany during the closing month of World War II and two were handed over to Canadian authorities. Today the aircraft belong to the National Aviation Museum in Ontario. This plane carried the production number 191 095 and was formerly flown by pilots of JG 400 in combat. The camouflage seems to be very authentic and shows a late war conversion of the rocket-powered *Komet* painted mid-1944.

Above: Another Me 163 captured by Allied forces near Leipzig. It was possibly an experimental aircraft of *Erprobungskommando* 16 which included some twenty Me 163B-0s and B-1s. A few Me 163A experimentals formerly used by *Erprobungskommando* 16 were handed over to JG 400 to continue flying at Brandis. The aircraft later was blown up by a couple of hand grenades put into the main fuselage section. The upper surfaces show a standard splinter camouflage used by nearly all aircraft belonging I./JG 400.

Below: This photograph belongs to a number of very rare colour pictures of JG 400's last rocket fighters after their capture by American ground forces in 1944 and 1945. Before it fell into Allied hands, German soldiers destroyed this Me 163B-1 together with many others. After a short struggle, the 69th US Infantry Division took the last operational rocket fighter base at Brandis but most of the aircraft captured were wrecks.

Above and right: An Me 163B-1 at an unknown location. A pilot's emblem can be discerned on the right side of the fuselage. On a red shield outlined in yellow is written '*Die schwarze 13*', 'Black 13', implying that the enemy under attack would have only a small chance to escape. Possibly the pilot had a different opinion. Note the thick armoured glass panel at the front of the cockpit and leather-covered headrest. After its capture, US soldiers used the emblem for target practice.

Above and below: Two views of a model showing the projected development of the Me 163 which was intended to receive the new designation Ju 248. There are known no colour photographs of the Ju 248 rocket fighters. But the well-made model built by Günter Sengfelder gives a good impression of the improved Me 163. By April 1945 it had only undertaken some flights as a glider with the help of a towing aircraft belonging to the Junkers works.

Right: One of the first wind-tunnel models of the successor to the Me 163, the Me 263. The new design featured some improvements over the Me 163B-1, including a fully retractable undercarriage which allowed easier handling on the ground and avoided a difficult recovery after the pilots returned from a mission. Furthermore, larger fuel tanks allowed a greater combat range.

Left: A close-up view of BP 20 M16 at the evaluation area on the Heuberg Military Training Ground which belonged to the *Wehrmacht*. Two different launch sites were constructed on the Ochsenkopf mountain by early 1945. The first metal construction was built mid-November 1944 and was used a few days later. The M16 is painted all-over RLM grey with two red stripes around the fuselage.

This Ba 349A-0 is stored at the Silverhill facility. The aircraft belonged to a small batch of pre-production aircraft and was fitted with a nose-mounted R4M *Batterie* (small air-to-air rockets). The wings of this aircraft were sawn off because there was not enough room in the storage hangar. The *Natter* urgently awaits restoration for possible display of this outstanding aircraft.

A close-up view of one of the *Natter* aircraft captured by Allied forces at Sankt Leonhard in Austria at the end of World War II. The workmanship appears to have been good but the materials used were cheap quality. After combat, the part shown here was jettisoned and recovered by a parachute. The pilot and rear part of the fuselage were also equipped with parachutes for a safe return to earth.

Right: The Opel-Hatry Rak 1 was one of the first attempts to enter a new era of aviation. This small experimental aircraft was designed by a former glider student from the Rhön-Rossiten *Gesellschaft* and was propelled by sixteen solid-fuel rockets fixed in the rear part of the cockpit gondola. The flights were carried out near Frankfurt am Main. Additional test installations of a rocket engine in an aircraft fuselage were carried out by Valier and Espenlaub.

Below: The aircraft was launched from a rail fixed on the ground. There was only a short period of enthusiasm. Fritz von Opel, who sponsored the project, lost interest in the trials and in an improved project based on Rak 1 shortly after the experimental aircraft crashed. All future plans for installing rockets of greater thrust in an aircraft were abandoned because von Opel developed a greater interest in rocket-powered cars and other projects.

Above: Without the experience gained from the evaluation of the DFS 194 it would have been impossible to proceed with more powerful designs, the Me 163 and the enlarged version called Me 263. During the first phase of flight evaluation the prototype was tested without its own propulsion and was flown as a normal glider. Important data on the flight behaviour of delta aircraft was gathered during these tests. This was important for the construction of the later Me 163.

Below: The installation of a 400 kp rocket engine developed by Helmut Walter to propel the DFS 194 experimental aircraft. This rocket engine was followed by several more advanced designs which were tested after April 1936, achieving a static thrust of 1,000 kp. There were many attempts up to the end of the war to improve the performance of the Walter and BMW engines. Finally a thrust of more than 1,500 kp was reported during static tests. A second but smaller combustion chamber was intended to produce a higher output.

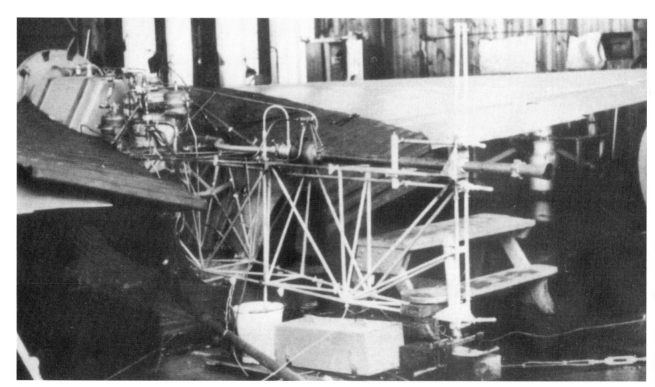

Above: Heini Dittmar belonged to a group of young but well-known and very experienced glider pilots engaged in the evaluation of many flying-wing designs. Here, before taking off with the help of a rocket engine, he dons a special protective overall. A small hangar, where maintenance work would have been carried out, can be seen in the background. The fuel components of all German rocket engines were very dangerous to handle. Many people were killed or injured when both components of the liquid-fuel engines unintentionally came into contact.

Below: After his return Heini Dittmar reports on the data gathered about the flight behaviour to some waiting DFS engineers. The experimental aircraft was unpainted and showed neither civil nor military markings. The aircraft has been fitted with three different pitot tubes on the forward fuselage, some 3 ft above the nose-cone.

Above: A rear view of the DFS 194 whose rear fuselage was jacked up on a small trolley to move the experimental aircraft back to its hangar. Note the tank for the special fuel on the boot of the open touring car in the background. To avoid unwelcome spectators the evaluation was carried out on a secure airfield near the Baltic Sea. Besides being conducted at the Peenemünde proving ground, rocket aircraft development was also pushed forward at Karlshagen some miles away where many laboratories were built in dense woods quite near the shores.

Opposite page, top: Possibly at Peenemünde, the later experimental site for testing nearly all kind of missiles and rocket propelled aircraft, this view of the DFS 194 was taken during summer 1940. The work on this aircraft was a success and allowed Alexander Lippisch and the Messerschmitt works to start work on the most secret 'project X', the way to the Me 163, a single-seat rocket fighter with an outstanding climb-rate but a poor range.

Right: The first experimental Me 163 (KE+SW) painted all over in RLM grey was designated Me 163A V4. The original Bf 163 was an unsuccessful pre-war light aircraft design which did not progress beyond the prototype stage. In an effort to disguise the true nature of its new rocket fighter, Messerschmitt was ordered to re-use the defunct 163 number rather than use a new number.

Above: Heini Dittmar in the small cabin of the first Me 163 experimental aircraft which was flown at Peenemünde during summer 1941. Initially the aircraft was flown as a glider until the first engine trials by a Kiel-based firm called

Walter had been passed. Due to severe problems with engine development it took many months before the engines were reliable. Many explosions were reported before the combustion chambers were of the desired standard.

Left: A Me 163A during transportation by *Reichsbahn* to the *Erprobungsstelle* (*E-Stelle*, or evaluation centre) at Rechlin. At least ten aircraft belonging to the A series were built. After they had passed this stage of evaluation most of the Me 163As were used as training aircraft for young rocket-fighter pilots before they took on the more powerful Me 163B. To transfer the rocket aircraft to other places a *Staffel* equipped with Bf 110 tug aircraft was needed. The second task of this unit was to tow the unpowered Me 163s to train new pilots.

Above and Below: Two views of the accident which happened during the secret demonstration of the fifth prototype at Peenemünde on 25 August 1942. The aircraft formerly showed the code GG+EA and had been transferred to Peenemünde on 8 November 1941 to evaluate its flight performance and behaviour as a glider. After Walter succeeded in April 1942 in providing a reliable rocket engine several powered trials were conducted and the aircraft showed good flight characteristics.

Above and below: The Me 163B V21 (W.Nr. 16310030) shown flew with the markings VA+SS. The aircraft was used for several evaluation missions to test an improved landing gear. During summer 1943 a 'hot engine' (HWK 109-509 B) was installed. From 24 June 1943 the aircraft was used for high-performance flights. The aircraft, painted over-all RLM grey, was fitted with an armament consisting of two heavy MG 151/20 guns and a complete wireless operation system. A modern gunsight was installed in front of the armoured glass plate in front of the pilot.

Right: The development department and the production lines of the Me 163's HWK 109-509 (R II-211) were situated at Kiel in northern Germany. In the rear part of the Walter works three test stands can be seen. In the large complex several other developments were carried out. Besides the engines to be installed in all kinds of rocket fighters secret torpedoes and JATO (jet-assisted take-off) systems were planned and later built in large quantities.

Below: After removal of the rear part of the fairings the rocket engine together with the rear part of the combustion chamber can be seen. The first R II-211 was installed in the Me 163B V2 for static testing in mid-1943. By June 1943 the experimental jet fighter was ready for the first 'sharp' take-off which was carried out by Rudolf Opitz on 24 June 1943. Opitz was a very experienced glider pilot during the 1930s and was, together with Heini Dittmar, well known to all young flyers of the *Luftwaffe*.

Left: The Me 163B V21 here was painted all-over RLM grey. The aircraft was tested by Rudolf Opitz on 31 July 1943. In order to record all data of rocket engine operation and performance, a camera was fixed on Opitz's head to take views of the instrument panel during the flight tests. The photograph also shows an improved skid which was altered after failures in early tests. Due to poor installation of the pilot's seat and flexibility of the skid, a few pilots had been injured during landing their Me 163s.

Left: This Me 163B-0 formerly belonged to *Erprobungskommando* 16 based at Zwischenahn near Oldenburg. It was destroyed by German forces by the end of the war. The aircraft was painted all-over RLM grey. The aircraft was possibly only used for training purposes because neither the two MG 151/20 nor the two MK 108 had been installed. Because no markings are visible it is not possible to identify the aircraft shown.

Above: The first combat-ready Me 163B, the V14, was evaluated at the *Luftwaffe* base at Zwischenahn near Oldenburg by pilots of the *Erprobungskommando* 16. The aircraft was first tested by the very experienced Rudolf Opitz. During the first trials it climbed at 740 kph after the dolly had been jettisoned only seconds after the aircraft left the ground. When the release system failed, fatal accidents were inevitable.

Right: The 'White 5', an Me 163B-1, one of the target-defence fighters belonging to EK 16, shown in this picture was part of the first seventy machines produced by the Messerschmitt works in Bavaria. The large skid beneath the fuselage was readjusted with the rear lower than usual in order to line up only with the tail wheel. An MG 151/20 or an MK 108 could be fixed in each wing root. The development department of Messerschmitt was also employed in testing the operational use of other weapons, especially small unguided missiles.

Left: Shortly after taking off the pilot released the jettisonable undercarriage and climbed with a constant speed of more than 600 kph to reach high-flying targets in the sky over Germany. The ground crew then collected the dollies along the runway. The aircraft commencing a 'sharp' start shown here belonged to EK 16 based at the *Luftwaffe* base at Zwischenahn which was surrounded with dense forests.

Below: It was difficult for the *Erprobungskommando* 16 to move its small rocket fighters until special recovery trucks were provided by the *Luftwaffe*. At first inflatable bags were used to raise the rocket fighter in order to attach the aircraft to a dolly. Later a special recovery system, as shown here, was used for retrieving the Me 163s serving with *Luftwaffe* front-line fighter units.

Above: A close-up taken at Zwischenahn where an Me 163B-1 has just been taken back to its hangar for a check-up before flying another combat mission. Compared with later jet fighters able to taxi under their own power the use of rocket fighters without the help of special equipment was believed to be very ineffective due to the huge effort necessary on the ground which only allowed a few missions per day.

Below: On concrete runways it was quite possible to tow an Me 163 rocket fighter on its own dolly with the help of the *Scheuch-Schlepper* alone. These trucks were used to move the Me 163s to the starting area, and the maintenance or engine test hangars at Zwischenahn, Venlo or Brandis. The 'White 14' being moved was one of the aircraft mainly used as a trainer for new rocket pilots. Often one of the former Me 163A experimental aircraft were used for training purposes due to the lack of newer aircraft.

Above: One of EK 16's Me 163B-1s taking off at Zwischenahn during Winter 1944. A few seconds later the pilot will release the small jettisonable undercarriage. The aircraft was well camouflaged to be hidden in the woods nearby without much extra effort. The taking off and landing phases were protected by several 20 mm gun positions situated around the base. Many of these were manned by members of the *Hitlerjugend* (Hitler Youth), trained by older AA personnel.

Below: Alignment of the aircraft for take-off was done manually at the starting position. Some five members of the ground crew were needed to fulfill this task. The photograph is believed to have been taken during summer 1944 at Zwischenahn. Note the well-camouflaged fuselage of this Me 163B-1 which was part of I./JG 400. It was the first *Gruppe* of the sole rocket fighter *Geschwader* established by 1944. First only two units, the 1./JG 400 and the 2./JG 400, together with *Erprobungskommando* 16, were engaged in countering Allied bomber formations over north-western Germany. They had minor success.

Above: A Me 163B-1, possibly used by 2./JG 400 in Brandis in 1944, shows the late camouflage scheme designed to conceal the small aircraft while on the ground from Allied reconnaissance pilots who monitored all known bases where German high-tech aircraft had been reported. The aircraft of the second *Staffel* of the rocket-fighter *Geschwader* is recognisable by a yellow nose section.

Right: After testing the rocket engine of an Me 163 it was necessary to wash out the motor parts in the back of the fuselage to remove all traces of the highly explosive *T-Stoff* and *C-Stoff* (components of the liquid fuel) and avoid catastrophic mixing of the two. During these tests, carried out periodically to be certain that no Me 163 would explode, the local fire brigade of the *Luftwaffe* was present. But despite all precautions explosions occurred and cost the *Luftwaffe* many members of the ground crew and experienced pilots.

Above: At Zwischenahn this Me 163B-1 of EK 16 awaits its next start. Alongside the aircraft is a battery cart connected during the final checks on the liquid-fuel rocket engine to save electricity. On the rear part of the fighter's fuselage a 'C' on a yellow background told the maintenance crew where to fill the *C-Stoff*. On the main fuselage section a 'T' for *T-Stoff* was painted to avoid dangerous mistakes when filling the fuel compartments before taking off.

Left: *Feldwebel* Rolf 'Bubi' Glogner preparing for a flight at Zwischenahn with one of EK 16's Me 163B-1s. Later the leather clothing was replaced by a synthetic flying suit. This non-commissioned officer together with Hans Bolt, Fritz Kelb, Hartmuth Ryll and a few others belonged to a group of very experienced rocket fighter pilots trained by Heini Dittmar and Rudolf Opitz. The latter also initiated the more senior officers who were chosen to take over the command of rocket fighter *Staffeln* or *Gruppen*.

Opposite page, top: One of the most famous *Komet* pilots, Rudolf 'Pitz' Opitz entering his Me 163B-1 at Zwischenahn. He wears a flight suit, special boots and gloves all made from non-organic materials to prevent his being burned in the event of an accident, a direct hit on the rocket motor or a belly landing after his mission.

Opposite page, bottom: At the secret research establishment at Peenemünde situated on the island of Usedom on the shores of the Baltic, this experimental system was tested to accelerate an Me 163 with a rocket sled fitted with two rocket engines at the back. A non-flying model of the Me 163 which was nearly the same size and weight as the Me 163 was fixed on the sled. The tests were aborted because of the amount of thrust required to launch the aircraft was excessive.

Above: This photo was taken at the *Luftwaffe* base at Brandis in April or May 1945. Several destroyed Me 163s were found here after German forces had demolished as many as possible before the first Allied soldiers arrived. The Me 163 in the centre is believed to be the B V45 (W.Nr.163100055, PK+QP) flown as tactical '05'. In the background the fragments of the experimental Hs 130A V1 can be recognised.

Above: The wooden mock-up of the Me 263 fell into Soviet hands at the end of the war. The well-made model of the second Messerschmitt rocket fighter was built by Junkers who took over the development of the new fighter aircraft because of lack of capacity at Messerschmitt who were fully occupied in trying to boost the flight endurance of the Me 262 jet fighter. Despite all the work invested there was never any real hope of introducing an improved rocket fighter, for example the Me 263 (Ju 248), because the war was nearly over.

Above: Another, three-quarters frontal view of the 1 : 1 scale wooden mock-up of the Me 263. Only the wing roots have been built to show the fairings of the main undercarriage. The series wings were built separately and tested in flight. The antennas of the FuG 16 ZY and other wireless systems can be seen on the spine of the model. The mock-up was captured by the Allies. To prevent it falling into Soviet hands, American soldiers destroyed many components in the region of Dessau and Brandis during a few days in summer 1945.

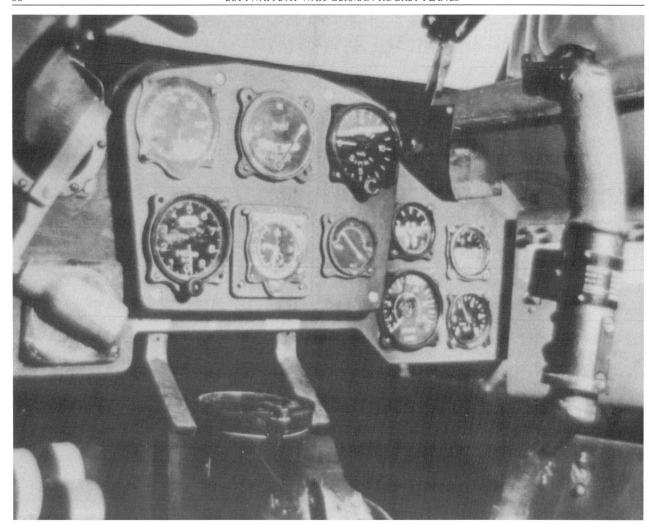

Above: The cockpit of the Me 263 target-defence fighter was built as a wooden mock-up to check the positions of all the instruments and the general equipment necessary for combat. In the centre, there is a panel housing the six main flight instruments. The engine controls were situated on the left. The compass was placed beneath the main panel.

Left: The wooden mock-up of the engine controls of the later Me 163A-1 target-defence fighter worked out by Messerschmitt and under revision by specialists working for Junkers. Due to the improved propulsion, two different combustion chambers were proposed which could be handled separately. In order to save expensive fuel there was a *Marschtriebwerk* (the cruise powerplant, an auxiliary cruise chamber of 400 kp thrust) near the main propulsion unit of some 2,000 kp thrust.

Right: Two huge MK 108 cannon were fitted inside the wing roots. When building the mock-up, real MK 108s were used to check the installation. The guns were estimated to have forty rounds each. Due to the firepower of two MK 108s it proved possible to destroy a heavy four-engined Allied bomber with one or two hits. Later it was supposed to use air-to-air missiles under both wings. First tests of the R4M rockets were undertaken with a modified Me 163A.

Below: Besides the development of the C and D models of the Me 163, and the Me 263, there were other variants built between 1944 and April 1945 to test new components. One of the experimental aircraft was this one. It is believed to be a lengthened Me 163B fitted with a non-retractable undercarriage. Due to the lack of parts it was difficult to make progress with the prototypes.

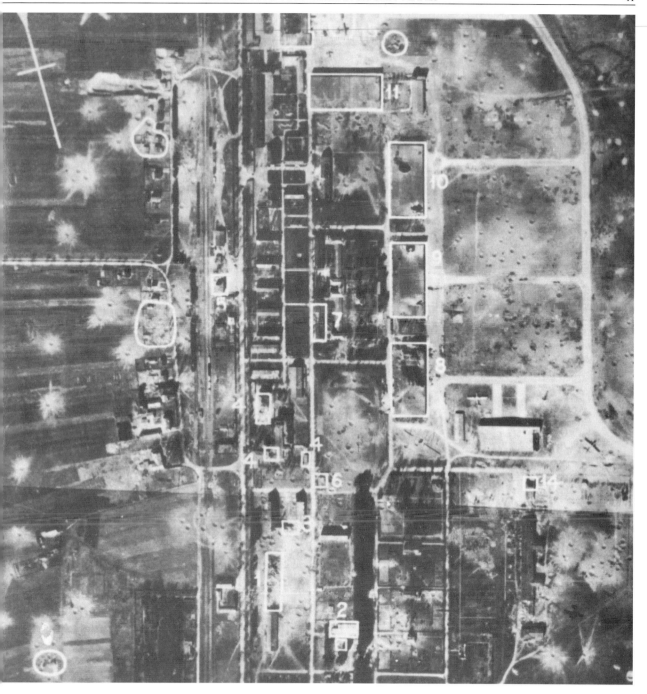

Opposite page, top: The first experimental Me 263A-1 fighter, the Ju 248 V1, was completed early in 1945. After the roll-out in March 1945, due to construction problems, it was still without an engine when the war ended. It was used to complete the general equipment layout. The main gear was not retractable because of missing hydraulic cylinders. At the end of the war, between three and five other Me 263 prototypes had been assembled near Dessau.

Opposite page bottom: The initial flight evaluation of the Ju 248 V1 was carried out by towing it as a glider. To measure the wind flow, wool tufts were glued on the wings and the fin section. There is no evidence that the Ju 248 V1 was ever flown with its own rocket engine before the unconditional surrender

in May 1945. Much of the data from the development of the Me 263 was captured by the Americans and was later taken by Soviet ground forces when areas captured by the Western Allies became part of the Soviet Zone.

Above: Besides work on the *Komet* and the Bachem *Natter*, the Messerschmitt works at Lechfeld tried to produce a more powerful aircraft combining the advantages of a rocket aircraft with those of a jet fighter. Initially, the development was called Interceptor I to III, but these aircraft later became part of the *Heimatschützer* (home defence fighter) programme. Due to Allied air raids attempts to complete these aircraft failed. Poor weather conditions and the lack of spare parts also prevented Messerschmitt from achieving much.

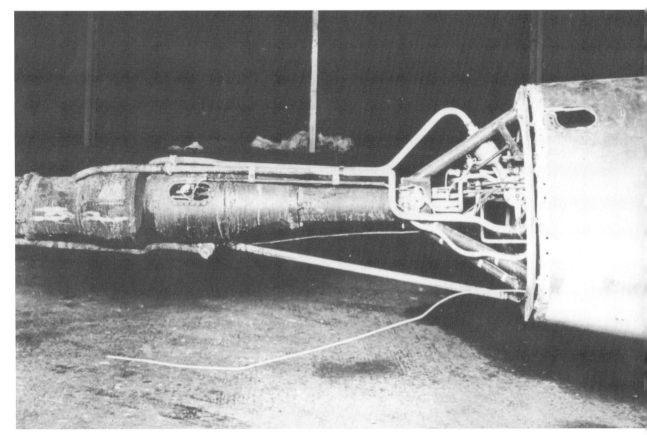

Left: The Me 262C-1a (W.Nr. 130186) during evaluation with an additional liquid-fuel installation in the rear fuselage. The picture was taken early in 1945 and shows the aircraft at Lager-Lechfeld some 30 km south of Augsburg in Bavaria. During the first flight tests only the two Jumo 004B jets were used. The first take-off with the addition of the rocket motor occurred before 27 February 1945. The aircraft was damaged beyond repair by fighter-bomber attack in March 1945.

Opposite page, top: A close-up view of the rocket engine fitted in the rear section of the Me 262C-1a's fuselage. A lot of technical problems had to be solved before the first 'sharp runnings' could be carried out by Messerschmitt pilots. The engine was handed over to the RAF for further evaluation after the end of the war. The fuselage of the Me 262 V186 was scrapped at Lechfeld because it was not needed further.

Below: The second attempt to create a so-called TLR (*Turbinenluftstrahltriebwerk mit Raketenantrieb* – a turbojet and rocket motor) fighter led to the Me 262C-2b. This TLR was tested at Lechfeld. The development was started early in summer 1942 when specialists from the BMW works at Allach invented a way to increase the power of jet aircraft by installing a rocket motor on their series BMW 003A-1 jet. The combined engine, the BMW 003R, was fitted in the *Heimatschützer* II by Messerschmitt during summer 1943.

Opposite page: A close-up view of one of the first engine systems being prepared for installation under the wings of a few Me 262s. Due to many technical defects there was no chance to begin static tests before January 1945. A few weeks earlier, on 20 December 1944, the first Me 262A-1a proposed for conversion to an experimental TLR fighter, designated the Me 262 V074, was delivered.

Above: On 25 January 1945 the right combustion chamber of the first experimental C-2b (W.Nr. 170074) exploded during a static test while the aircraft was standing in front of one of the huge hangars. The back part of the aircraft caught fire and the camouflage paint was burned off. The

BMW 003R engine was extensively damaged and it became necessary to change the engine and rebuild parts of the rear wing. Fortunately there were no causalities.

Below: After a new TLR unit was delivered from Munich a series of trials followed during February 1945 to check all systems of both engines. This testing revealed pressure problems as well as faulty electrical wiring. Therefore specialists from Allach (BMW) were ordered to investigate the BMW 003Rs being held at Lechfeld. Further difficulties arose with the Riedel starters and other systems. After having checked all parts of the BMW 003Rs, a first take-off was expected at end of February or early in March 1945.

Left: Factory pilot Lindner standing on the wing of the first Me 262C-2b which took off for the first time on 26 March 1945 at Lechfeld. Note the outlet above the exhaust cone of the BMW 003 jet where the BMW P 3395 rocket was situated. The bracket beneath the front of the cockpit is where a camera was to be fixed to film the rocket-assisted take-offs. Later the shortage of B4 fuel needed for the two BMW 003s led to their being removed late in March 1945 to be converted to take J2 fuel.

Below and opposite page, top: When American ground forces occupied the test centre, the Me 262 V074 was found without TLR engines. These had been removed because Germany's deteriorating situation in April 1945 meant that flight development of the target-defence fighter could not continue. Because there was no interest in the aircraft it was parked together with Me 262 V10 (W.Nr. 130005, VI+AE) in a space between damaged hangars in the western part of Lechfeld.

Opposite page, bottom: A last view of the former Me 262 target-defence fighter before it was scrapped on Allied orders. Plans to introduce a Me 262A-1a with a jettisonable fairing housing a Walter HWK 509 A-2 rocket motor placed beneath the fighter's fuselage were abandoned in April 1945. Three prototypes of the Me 262C-3a (*Heimatschützer* IV) were to be built but none was completed at the war's end. A few of the large jettisonable containers intended to be filled with *C-Stoff* and *T-Stoff* were captured at Oberammergau.

Opposite page, top: Besides the Me 163 there were plans to introduce several other rocket-powered target-defence fighters. By the end of 1944 Heinrich Himmler managed to take over the *Natter* project whose initial designs had been ordered by *Oberstleutnant* Siegfried Knemeyer who had been at the Development Office of the Technical Air Armaments Branch since August 1944. On his orders, several wind-tunnel tests had been initiated.

Opposite page, bottom: Flight development was carried out at the *Luftwaffe* base at Neuburg on the Danube at the end of 1944. In front of the first *Natter*, BP 20 M1, pilots of the *Deutsche Forschungsanstalt für Segelflug* (DFS or German Gliding Research Institute) together with members of the Bachem works discuss future tests. Left to right: Willy Fiedler (Bachem), unknown (Bachem), Hermann Zitter (DFS) and Erich Klöckner (DFS).

Below: The first stages of flight development were drawn up on 4 September 1944. Because it was proposed to introduce a *Natter* which the pilot flew in the prone position, the B9 of the *Deutsche Versuchsanstalt für Luftfahrt* (DVL) and a so-called *Liegekranich* were chosen for the first flights. After the arrangement of the seat was altered a few week later – as seen in the picture of BP 20 M1 – the plans were abandoned.

Opposite page, top: Another view showing the BP 20 M1 on 3 November 1944, taken prior to the first towed take-off by an He 111H-6 belonging to the DFS. The flight was filmed by the crew of a Ju 87 (BR+EZ) positioned behind the *Natter* which was fixed on a tricycle dolly constructed by Bachem. The M1 did not have an engine.

Opposite page, bottom: The BP 20 M1 was completed on 4 October 1944 but was not tested before early November 1944 at Neuburg. The mechanics have just fixed towing cables to the BP 20 M1's wings. After a short flight in which its longitudinal stability was tested the aircraft was released. The prototype was completely destroyed when it crashed near Neuburg.

Above: The unarmed He 111H-6 together with the BP 20 M1 experimental aircraft about to take off. The pilot, Hermann Zitter, the wireless operator, August Lohfink, and Erich Klöckner stand beside the He 111 (DG+RN) discussing the proposed test flight and the poor weather conditions.

Below: The instrument panel of the first *Natter* prototype which only had a speed indicator, the release for the rescue parachutes, and an intercommunication system which connected the *Natter*'s pilot with *Flugkapitän* Zitter and his crew flying the He 111H-6. The crank handle in the middle of the panel was needed to move the ballast fitted in the nose of the prototype. In front of the panel is the small control stick.

Left: After the first trial in November 1944 the third *Natter* was prepared as the second flyable prototype to be tested at Neuburg. The aircraft had a flight weight of 740 kg and was fitted with a fixed tricycle undercarriage to continue the evaluation of flight characteristics. But after landing at Neuburg the pilot stated that the flight behaviour was influenced by the fixed undercarriage.

Opposite page, bottom: A close-up view of the speed brakes installed at the back of the BP 20 M3's fuselage. After the pilot succeeded in landing causing only minor damage the aircraft was prepared to continue flying with a repaired undercarriage. The wires leading to the rear fuselage section were needed to release the emergency parachute located there. The workmanship appears to have been poorer than it might have been because of lack of time and cheap materials.

Below: The unmanned BP 20 M7 experimental aircraft was tested on 5 December 1944 after simultaneous trials with M5 and M6 on 2 December 1944 had been carried out. The fuselage of the M7 suffered only minor damage although the second recovery parachute was lost during its release. The fuselage was estimated to be ready for use for further static tests by Bachem works not later than early 1945.

Above: The first vertical launch trial using the BP 20 M21 had failed on 8 December 1944 after the aircraft burned because it did not became airborne due to technical faults in the electrical system. The second experimental aircraft to lift off from the vertical launching site at the Neuburg near the small town Stetten am kalten Markt was the BP 20 M16 which became available on 22 December 1944. The aircraft was fitted with only four boosters.

Left and opposite page, top: The BP 20 M16 lifting off from the ramp on 22 December 1944. It reached operating altitude powered by four booster rockets called *Schubgeräte* 34 (SG, thrust devices) which delivered a constant thrust of 1,200 kp. Left of the ramp is a crane which was used in the installation of the launch site. The unmanned experimental crashed after reaching horizontal flight and was completely destroyed when it hit the frozen ground on the Heuberg plateau.

Right: A close-up of the mock-up of the SG 34 installation on the left side of the BP 20's wooden fuselage built at Waldsee. The wooden dummies showed the size of the Schmidding-built take-off booster rockets used in the vertical take-off trials. Most of the BP 20s tested at the Heuberg lifted off with these boosters. Only three to five *Natter* aircraft took-off with the help of the SG 34 and these were also fitted with a complete Hans-Walter-Kiel (HWK) liquid-fuel rocket motor, the 109-509 A-2, of which a few were dumped into Lake Waldsee.

Above: Dipl-Ing. Erich Bachem, who formerly worked for Fieseler at Kassel, built up his own business from the factory site that had previously belonged to a group of smaller firms which built aircraft parts for Dornier at Friedrichshafen at Lake Constance. After supporting the Do 335 programme, he came up with a number of proposals including an armoured manned rocket for use as a *Mistel* built from laminates and sheet metal and propelled by a solid rocket motor inside a laminated rear fuselage. Later, during summer 1944, this turned into a single-seat target-defence fighter called the *Natter*.

Right: A view of the BP 20 M17 only a few minutes before taking off. In front of the launch site, Willy Fiedler and two other specialists are discussing the next trial. On the top of the launching tower, another member of the evaluation team is working on the launching system which could be turned. Note the interesting red markings painted on both wings to observe the rotation of the aircraft when it took off.

Above and right: On 29 December 1944 the BP 20 M17 took off. After the prototype left the guidance ramp the aircraft rose to a height at which the recovery parachute was activated too late. Consequently the forward fuselage section broke away. All of these tests were filmed by Bachem's employees, officials from the *Oberkommando der Luftwaffe* (OKL) or the SS. During the trial of the M16, the malfunction of the parachute had been visible. The forward section of the aircraft, which was mostly undamaged during recovery, was reconstructed and used for static testing at Waldsee early in 1945. Many of these tests were undertaken to improve the installation of the rocket motor and the general layout of the armament in the nose section.

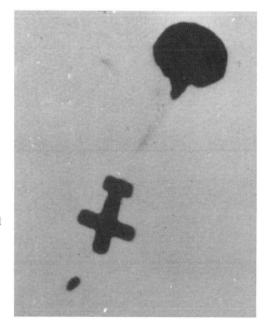

Left: On 25 February 1945 the BP 20 M22 was prepared for take-off. The launch of M22 and M23 was probably filmed by a member of *SS Sonderkommando* N to inform the *Reichsführer SS* Heinrich Himmler and *SS-Gruppenführer* (General of *Waffen SS*) Dr-Ing. Hans Kammler. Therefore the SS personnel posed in correct uniforms and handled the new 'wonder weapon'. The unmanned aircraft shown, launched on 25 February 1945, was the first experimental aircraft fitted with a Walter liquid-fuel rocket motor.

Right: Under the personal supervision of Willy Fiedler the well-camouflaged BP 20 M23 experimental fighter is prepared for a first manned take-off at the Ochsenkopf. After several static tests with the Walter liquid-fuel motor and under the direct orders of both *Oberkommando der Luftwaffe* and *SS-Reichswirtschaftshauptamt* Erich Bachem himself encouraged a manned take-off as soon as possible. But technical and logistic problems prevented a factory pilot undertaking the important test earlier than March 1945.

Left: *Gefreiter* Lothar Sieber, born on 7 April 1922 in Dresden, and Gertrud Nauditt were engaged to be married. He became a pilot of the secret KG 200 and flew a lot of different *Luftwaffe* aircraft and captured aircraft, including SM 79s, TB 3s and B-17s. On 24 April 1942 he was promoted *Leutnant* but he lost his rank on 11 February 1943 by the sentence of the *Feldgericht* Minsk (martial court of Minsk). On 22 December 1944 he became the factory pilot of the Bachem *Werke* at Waldsee and was present when the first *Natter* was tested at the Ochsenkopf. He was a very experienced pilot and prepared himself at the end of February 1945 to be the first soldier of the *Luftwaffe* to carry out a vertical take-off.

Opposite page, top:
During the preliminary work on the launching ramp, four men were needed to 'load the ramp' with the next *Natter* (BP 20 M23) with the help of a crank drive fixed at the back of the ramp. Possibly the personnel belonged to the *Sonderkommando* of the *Waffen SS* commanded by *SS-Hauptsturmführer* (captain) Heinz Flessner who supported Erich Bachem's work with at least three SS officers, some fifteen *SS-Scharführer* (NCOs) and some 150 SS men. Most of these were former front-line soldiers who had been wounded and were used for industrial duties working in their former professions.

Above: Henry Bethpeder and the factory pilot, Lothar Sieber, standing in front of BP 20 M23 which was ready for take-off on 1 march 1945. His pilot's log offered a lot of flight experience. When serving with KG 200 Sieber was believed to be a very successful pilot, able to control any kind of aircraft in any situation. Because he was a member of the KG 200 which was engaged in top secret missions the young pilot was known to the *SS-Reichssicherheitshauptamt* and eventually made contact with Erich Bachem.

Above: On the morning of 1 March 1945 *Gefreiter* Lothar Sieber tries to enter the small cockpit of his Bachem *Natter*. After igniting all of the boosters and the Walter rocket motor Sieber's *Natter* went faster and faster and disappeared in the dense grey clouds. It seems that problems arose after Lothar Sieber tried to maintain control over the aircraft. Possibly he lost orientation when passing through the clouds. He tried to bail out but one of his legs was trapped. At that moment the *Natter* hit the ground. He died in the crash.

Opposite page, bottom: The rocket battery in the nose was evaluated with this wooden fuselage of a Bachem *Natter*. In order to allow the exhaust gases from the twenty-four R4Ms to escape several designs were worked out. Finally, two air shutters on both sides of the forward fuselage were proposed. However, it was suggested by Bachem's engineers that openings behind the rocket battery would be better as it would be cheaper to produce a fuselage with two or more rows of slits behind the formidable rocket armament. A Revi 16 gunsight or an improved system was proposed by the Bachem development department.

Below: Until today it was said that Lothar Sieber broke his neck when the main canopy broke. The remains of the M 23 were dug up in 1998. Besides fragments of the engine several other parts were recovered with the help of the *Bundeswehr*. Near the debris the launching ramps were discovered. Due to local interest in the first vertical take-off by Lothar Sieber, a small museum will be established at Stetten am kalten Markt in southern Germany. Possibly a lot of the remains collected by *Oberstabsfeldwebel* Hensel will be shown there within the next two years.

Opposite page: Several different armament proposals for the *Natter* were under development between summer 1944 and March 1945. Field trials were carried out near to the launch site on the Ochsenkopf. Because all aspects of the *Natter* development were top secret only a few details have been reported until now. In addition to the use of a battery of twenty-four R4M rockets in the nose, as shown here, it was planned to install a launch tube firing 30 mm MK 108 cannon shells or two MK 108 in the forward nose section of the rocket fighter. Because there was no space under the small wings to install R4Ms the only place was the nose section.

Below: This rocket battery is believed to have been used in one of the static tests. It was reported that the practical evaluation of the R4M-*Waben* and other smaller unguided rockets, e.g. the *Föhn Batterie*, was first undertaken with tests on the ground. This launcher was built by Esslinger *Eisenwerke* near Stuttgart. The cheap launcher allowed information about the behaviour of the small rockets to be gathered in combat.

Above: During weapon testing at the Ochsenkopf this photo was taken by a member of the *Waffen-SS*. In the jettisonable nose section of the *Natter* the *Grosse Rohrblock* 108 is a *Schrotschusswaffe* (shotgun weapon) which could fire forty-eight MK 108 rounds into the target. Due to the formidable firepower of the MK 108 it was estimated that nearly every enemy contact with a *Natter* would lead to the destruction of an enemy aircraft. The *SS-Scharführer* is preparing the nose section to be fitted to the fuselage which is attached to a ground-rig.

Below: *SS Sonderkommando* N tried to evaluate the *Natter* as quickly as possible under poor conditions. The dangerous fuel was transported in milk churns from a farmhouse nearby. Note the 'T' on the white background on the churn in the centre. It took some time to assemble all the necessary vehicles and petrol. Because of shortages the development of the *Natter* was delayed more and more. There was not enough *T-Stoff* and *C-Stoff* nor rocket motors to complete all of the experimental *Nattern* and those of the pre-series.

Right: In April 1945 only two *Natter* launchings were undertaken. Until 5 April 1945 the *Sonderkommando* N of the SS together with specialists from the Bachem works had achieved twelve vertical take-offs to check the flight behaviour of the new fighter. Only two more flights of a *Natter* occurred between early April and the end of the evaluation on the Heuberg. The aircraft shown here is believed to be the second pre-series aircraft (BP 20 M52).

Left: This is possibly the BP 20 M52 being brought into launch position. Four different symbols have been painted on upper and lower wing surfaces in order to record all movements after launch. The new but very cheap launch ramp was constructed very simply. Only massive pine trees, some minor wooden components and a few other parts made from iron were used to make *Natter* launch sites in what remained of unoccupied Germany.

Opposite page, top: A German evaluation site early in April 1945. The last *Natter* (M52) was launched from a wooden ramp near a little wood on the Ochsenkopf mountain at the Heuberg military area. The fuel was transported by horse- or oxen-drawn vehicles. It was the same situation at Ohrdruf in central Germany where another launch site was established. Another *Natter* evaluation was carried out near Karlshagen on the island of Usedom.

Opposite page, bottom: Erich Bachem with the head of the *Truppenübungsplatz* Neuburg, *General* Besch and his personal adjutant early in 1945. Bachem reported the newest results concerning the *Natter* development to the *General*. A few days earlier the BP 20 M23, M24 and M33 were tested near the Ochsenkopf mountain. One of these, the M33 was completely destroyed at an altitude of some 800 m after one of the boosters exploded. The M23 ended its test flight far earlier than estimated. Both M23 and M24 were two of the few *Natter* aircraft fitted with rocket motors.

Opposite page, top:
Several attempts were made to produce enough *Nattern* for a combat mission. '*Operation Krokus*' was first planned to take place near Stuttgart but enemy forces had reached the Wuerttemberg capital earlier than estimated. After the Allied forces had advanced nearly to Waldsee all necessary material was assembled to be sent to Bad Wörishofen and to the region of Füssen in Bavaria. Evaluation of the *Natter* was attempted at Wörishofen without any success. Only a few of the aircraft could be saved and transported there.

Left: Four *Nattern* were transported to Sankt Leonhard in the Pitztal Valley in Austria in April 1945. These were nearly completed but slightly damaged aircraft together with some spares and tools. Thirteen personnel connected with the BP 20 development accompanied them. Hans von Behr, who had a financial interest in the aircraft, the engineers Gerhard Schaller, Heinrich Hofmann, Henry Bethpeder, Heinz Flessner and Richard Granzow and two pilots, Hans Zuebert and Richard Eisenrigler, and a few others belonged to the *Natter* team. Most of the *Natter* aircraft were found on special lorries that were to be towed by trucks.

Above: '*Operation Krokus*' never took place. Despite some successful experiments carried out with the wooden launching ramp, there was no chance to enter the operational phase. There are reports which mentioned that all metal parts for the initial *Natter* attack were delivered, but there was no opportunity to produce enough aircraft and to instruct new pilots early in 1945. After it became obvious that there would be no chance to carry out the ambitious orders of the SS and the *Luftwaffe*, the operational *Natter* aircraft were transported to different places in the Tyrol and to the German Alps.

Above: One of the tasks of the combined intelligence teams of the Allies was to check all captured weapons which could be useful for their own future armament purposes. Therefore all parts of the *Natter* seemed to be of interest. The Allied specialists also captured documents at Sankt Leonhard, which described an MK 108 armament and details concerning the modifications of all variants of the *Natter*. Of the ultimate design, the Ba 349B-0, only drawings were captured because there had been no chance to build one of these aircraft.

Below: After capturing two repairable BP 20 built at Waldsee, two serviceable Walter engines (109-509 A-2), four SG (SR) 34 solid-fuel take-off rockets, four wings for BP 20 aircraft, two boxes of 7.3 cm rockets and several smaller parts were sent to Stuttgart by Allied intelligence officers for shipping to USA. There, one *Natter* was launched but the test failed. The aircraft hit a petrol station which was destroyed. The other *Natter* is still part of the Silverhill Collection of the NSAM in Washington DC.